Songs of Friendship by James Whitcomb Riley

Poet and author James Whitcomb Riley was born on October 7th 1849 in Greenfield, Indiana. Better known as the "Hoosier Poet" for his work with regional dialects, and also as the "Children's Poet" Riley was born into an influential and well off family.

However his education was spotty but he was surrounded by creativity which was to stand him in good stead later in life.

His early career was a series of low paid temporary jobs. After stints as a journalist and billboard proprietor he had the resources to dedicate more of his efforts to writing.

Riley was prone to drink which was to affect his health and later his career but after a slow start and a lot of submissions he began to gain traction first in newspapers and then with the publication of his dialect poems 'Boone County Poems' he came to national recognition. This propelled him to long term contracts to perform on speaking circuits. These were very successful but over the years his star waned.

In 1888 he was too drunk to perform and the ensuing publicity made everything seem very bleak for a while. However he overcame that and managed to re-negotiate his contracts so that he received his rightful share of the income and his wealth thereafter increased very quickly.

A bachelor, Riley seems to have his writings as his only outlet, and although in his public performances he was well received, his publications were becoming seen as banal and repetitive and sales of these later works began to fall away.

Eventually after his last tour in 1895 he retired to spend his final years in Indianapolis writing patriotic poetry.

Now in poor health, weakened by years of heavy drinking, Riley, the Hoosier Poet died on July 23, 1916 of a stroke. In a final, unusual tribute, Riley lay in state for a day in the Indiana Statehouse, where thousands came to pay their respects. Not since Lincoln had a public personage received such a send-off. He is buried at Crown Hill Cemetery in Indianapolis.

Index Of Poems
BACK FROM TOWN
A HOBO VOLUNTARY
BE OUR FORTUNES AS THEY MAY
I SMOKE MY PIPE
UNCLE SIDNEY TO MARCELLUS
A SONG BY UNCLE SIDNEY
THE POET'S LOVE FOR THE CHILDREN
FRIEND OF A WAYWARD HOUR
MY HENRY
A LETTER TO A FRIEND
THE OLD-FASHIONED BIBLE
GOOD-BY ER HOWDY-DO
WHEN WE THREE MEET

"THE LITTLE MAN IN THE TINSHOP"
TOMMY SMITH
TOM VAN ARDEN
OUR OLD FRIEND NEVERFAIL
MY BACHELOR CHUM
ART AND POETRY - TO HOMER DAVENPORT
DOWN TO THE CAPITAL
OLD CHUMS
SCOTTY
THE OLD MAN
JAMES B. MAYNARD
THE ANCIENT PRINTERMAN
THE OLD MAN AND JIM
THE OLD SCHOOL-CHUM
MY JOLLY FRIEND'S SECRET
IN THE HEART OF JUNE
THE OLD BAND
MY FRIEND
THE TRAVELING MAN
DAN O'SULLIVAN
MY OLD FRIEND
OLD JOHN HENRY
HER VALENTINE
CHRISTMAS GREETING
ABE MARTIN
THE LITTLE OLD POEM THAT NOBODY READS
IN THE AFTERNOON
BECAUSE
HERR WEISER
A MOTHER-SONG
WHAT "OLD SANTA" OVERHEARD
THE STEPMOTHER
WHEN OLD JACK DIED
THAT NIGHT
TO ALMON KEEFER - INSCRIBED IN "TALES OF THE OCEAN"
TO THE QUIET OBSERVER - AFTER HIS LONG SILENCE
REACH YOUR HAND TO ME
THE DEAD JOKE AND THE FUNNY MAN
AMERICA'S THANKSGIVING - 1900
OLD INDIANY - INTENDED FOR A DINNER OF THE INDIANA SOCIETY OF CHICAGO

James Whitcomb Riley – A Short Biography

TO YOUNG E. ALLISON - BOOKMAN
The bookman he's a humming-bird
His feasts are honey-fine,
(With hi! hilloo!
And clover-dew
And roses lush and rare!)

His roses are the phrase and word
Of olden tomes divine;
(With hi! and ho!
And pinks ablow
And posies everywhere!)
The Bookman he's a humming-bird,
He steals from song to song
He scents the ripest-blooming rhyme,
And takes his heart along
And sacks all sweets of bursting verse
And ballads, throng on throng.
(With ho! and hey!
And brook and brae,
And brinks of shade and shine!)

A humming-bird the Bookman is
Though cumbrous, gray and grim,
(With hi! hilloo!
And honey-dew
And odors musty-rare!)
He bends him o'er that page of his
As o'er the rose's rim.
(With hi! and ho!
And pinks aglow
And roses everywhere!)
Ay, he's the featest humming-bird,
On airiest of wings
He poises pendent o'er the poem
That blossoms as it sings
God friend him as he dips his beak
In such delicious things!
(With ho! and hey!
And world away
And only dreams for him!)

O friends of mine, whose kindly words come to me
Voiced only in lost lisps of ink and pen,
If I had power to tell the good you do me,
And how the blood you warm goes laughing through me,
My tongue would babble baby-talk again.

And I would toddle round the world to meet you
Fall at your feet, and clamber to your knees
And with glad, happy hands would reach and greet you,
And twine my arms about you, and entreat you
For leave to weave a thousand rhymes like these

A thousand rhymes enwrought of nought but presses
Of cherry-lip and apple-cheek and chin,
And pats of honeyed palms, and rare caresses,
And all the sweets of which as Fancy guesses

She folds away her wings and swoons therein.

BACK FROM TOWN

Old friends allus is the best,
Halest-like and heartiest:
Knowed us first, and don't allow
We're so blame much better now!
They was standin' at the bars
When we grabbed "the kivvered kyars"
And lit out fer town, to make
Money and that old mistake!

We thought then the world we went
Into beat "The Settlement,"
And the friends 'at we'd make there
Would beat any anywhere!
And they do fer that's their biz:
They beat all the friends they is
'Cept the raal old friends like you
'At staid at home, like I'd ort to!

W'y, of all the good things yit
I ain't shet of, is to quit
Business, and git back to sheer
These old comforts waitin' here
These old friends; and these old hands
'At a feller understands;
These old winter nights, and old
Young-folks chased in out the cold!

Sing "Hard Times'll come ag'in
No More!" and neighbors all jine in!
Here's a feller come from town
Wants that-air old fiddle down
From the chimbly! Git the floor
Cleared fer one cowtillion more!
It's poke the kitchen fire, says he,
And shake a friendly leg with me!

A HOBO VOLUNTARY

Oh, the hobo's life is a roving life;
It robs pretty maids of their heart's delight
It causes them to weep and it causes them to mourn
For the life of a hobo, never to return.

The hobo's heart it is light and free,
Though it's Sweethearts all, farewell, to thee!

Farewell to thee, for it's far away
The homeless hobo's footsteps stray.

In the morning bright, or the dusk so dim,
It's any path is the one for him!
He'll take his chances, long or short,
For to meet his fate with a valiant heart.

Oh, it's beauty mops out the sidetracked-car,
And it's beauty-beaut' at the pigs-feet bar;
But when his drinks and his eats is made
Then the hobo shunts off down the grade.

He camps near town, on the old crick-bank,
And he cuts his name on the water-tank
He cuts his name and the hobo sign,
"Bound for the land of corn and wine!"

(Oh, it's I like friends that he'ps me through,
And the friends also that he'ps you, too,
Oh, I like all friends, 'most every kind
But I don't like friends that don't like mine.)

There's friends of mine, when they gits the hunch,
Comes a swarmin' in, the blasted bunch,
"Clog-step Jonny" and "Flat-wheel Bill"
And "Brockey Ike" from Circleville.

With "Cooney Ward" and "Sikes the Kid"
And old "Pop Lawson" the best we had
The rankest mug and the worst for lush
And the dandiest of the whole blame push.

Oh, them's the times I remembers best
When I took my chance with all the rest,
And hogged fried chicken and roastin' ears, too,
And sucked cheroots when the feed was through.

Oh, the hobo's way is the railroad line,
And it's little he cares for schedule time;
Whatever town he's a-striken for
Will wait for him till he gits there.

And whatever burg that he lands in
There's beauties there just thick for him
There's beauty at "The Queen's Taste Lunch-stand," sure,
Or "The Last Chance Boardin' House" back-door.

He's lonesome-like, so he gits run in,
To git the hang o' the world ag'in;
But the laundry circles he moves in there

Makes him sigh for the country air,

So it's Good-by gals! and he takes his chance
And wads hisself through the workhouse-fence:
He sheds the town and the railroad, too,
And strikes mud roads for a change of view.

The jay drives by on his way to town,
And looks on the hobo in high scorn,
And so likewise does the farmhands stare
But what the haids does the hobo care!

He hits the pike, in the summer's heat
Or the winter's cold, with its snow and sleet
With a boot on one foot, and one shoe
Or he goes barefoot, if he chooses to.

But he likes the best, when the days is warm,
With his bum Prince-Albert on his arm
He likes to size up a farmhouse where
They haint no man nor bulldog there.

Oh, he gits his meals wherever he can,
So natchurly he's a handy man
He's a handy man both day and night,
And he's always blest with an appetite!

A tin o' black coffee, and a rhuburb pie
Be they old and cold as charity
They're hot-stuff enough for the pore hobo,
And it's "Thanks, kind lady, for to treat me so!"

Then he fills his pipe with a stub cigar
And swipes a coal from the kitchen fire,
And the hired girl says, in a smilin' tone,
"It's good-by, John, if you call that goin'!"

Oh, the hobo's life is a roving life,
It robs pretty maids of their heart's delight
It causes them to weep and it causes them to mourn
For the life of a hobo, never to return.

BE OUR FORTUNES AS THEY MAY
Be our fortunes as they may,
Touched with loss or sorrow,
Saddest eyes that weep to-day
May be glad to-morrow.

Yesterday the rain was here,

And the winds were blowing
Sky and earth and atmosphere
Brimmed and overflowing.

But to-day the sun is out,
And the drear November
We were then so vexed about
Now we scarce remember.

Yesterday you lost a friend
Bless your heart and love it!
For you scarce could comprehend
All the aching of it;

But I sing to you and say:
Let the lost friend sorrow
Here's another come to-day,
Others may to-morrow.

I SMOKE MY PIPE
I can't extend to every friend
In need a helping hand
No matter though I wish it so,
'Tis not as Fortune planned;
But haply may I fancy they
Are men of different stripe
Than others think who hint and wink,
And so I smoke my pipe!

A golden coal to crown the bowl
My pipe and I alone,
I sit and muse with idler views
Perchance than I should own:
It might be worse to own the purse
Whose glutted bowels gripe
In little qualms of stinted alms;
And so I smoke my pipe.

And if inclined to moor my mind
And cast the anchor Hope,
A puff of breath will put to death
The morbid misanthrope
That lurks inside as errors hide
In standing forms of type
To mar at birth some line of worth;
And so I smoke my pipe.

The subtle stings misfortune flings
Can give me little pain

When my narcotic spell has wrought
This quiet in my brain:
When I can waste the past in taste
So luscious and so ripe
That like an elf I hug myself;
And so I smoke my pipe.

And wrapped in shrouds of drifting clouds
I watch the phantom's flight,
Till alien eyes from Paradise
Smile on me as I write:
And I forgive the wrongs that live,
As lightly as I wipe
Away the tear that rises here;
And so I smoke my pipe.

UNCLE SIDNEY TO MARCELLUS

Marcellus, won't you tell us
Truly tell us, if you can,
What will you be, Marcellus,
When you get to be a man?

You turn, with never answer
But to the band that plays.
O rapt and eerie dancer,
What of your future days?

Far in the years before us
We dreamers see your fame,
While song and praise in chorus
Make music of your name.

And though our dreams foretell us
As only visions can,
You must prove it, O Marcellus,
When you get to be a man!

A SONG BY UNCLE SIDNEY

O were I not a clod, intent
On being just an earthly thing,
I'd be that rare embodiment
Of Heart and Spirit, Voice and Wing,
With pure, ecstatic, rapture-sent,
Divinely-tender twittering
That Echo swoons to re-present,
A bluebird in the Spring.

THE POET'S LOVE FOR THE CHILDREN

Kindly and warm and tender,
He nestled each childish palm
So close in his own that his touch was a prayer
And his speech a blessed psalm.

He has turned from the marvelous pages
Of many an alien tome
Haply come down from Olivet,
Or out from the gates of Rome

Set sail o'er the seas between him
And each little beckoning hand
That fluttered about in the meadows
And groves of his native land,

Fluttered and flashed on his vision
As, in the glimmering light
Of the orchard-lands of childhood,
The blossoms of pink and white.

And there have been sobs in his bosom,
As out on the shores he stept,
And many a little welcomer
Has wondered why he wept.

That was because, O children,
Ye might not always be
The same that the Savior's arms were wound
About, in Galilee.

FRIEND OF A WAYWARD HOUR

Friend of a wayward hour, you came
Like some good ghost, and went the same;
And I within the haunted place
Sit smiling on your vanished face,
And talking with your name.

But thrice the pressure of your hand
First hail congratulations and
Your last "God bless you!" as the train
That brought you snatched you back again
Into the unknown land.

"God bless me?" Why, your very prayer
Was answered ere you asked it there,
I know for when you came to lend

Me your kind hand, and call me friend,
God blessed me unaware.

MY HENRY

He's jes' a great, big, awk'ard, hulkin'
Feller, humped, and sort o' sulkin'
Like, and ruther still-appearin'
Kind-as-ef he wuzn't keerin'
Whether school helt out er not
That's my Henry, to a dot!

Allus kind o' liked him whether
Childern, er growed-up together!
Fifteen year' ago and better,
'Fore he ever knowed a letter,
Run acrosst the little fool
In my Primer-class at school.

When the Teacher wuzn't lookin',
He'd be th'owin' wads; er crookin'
Pins; er sprinklin' pepper, more'n
Likely, on the stove; er borin'
Gimlet-holes up thue his desk
Nothin' that boy wouldn't resk!

But, somehow, as I was goin'
On to say, he seemed so knowin',
Other ways, and cute and cunnin'
Allus wuz a notion runnin'
Thue my giddy, fool-head he
Jes' had be'n cut out fer me!

Don't go much on prophesyin',
But last night whilse I wuz fryin'
Supper, with that man a-pitchin'
Little Marthy round the kitchen,
Think-says-I, "Them baby's eyes
Is my Henry's, jes' p'cise!"

A LETTER TO A FRIEND

The past is like a story
I have listened to in dreams
That vanished in the glory
Of the Morning's early gleams;
And at my shadow glancing
I feel a loss of strength,
As the Day of Life advancing

Leaves it shorn of half its length.

But it's all in vain to worry
At the rapid race of Time
And he flies in such a flurry
When I trip him with a rhyme,
I'll bother him no longer
Than to thank you for the thought
That "my fame is growing stronger
As you really think it ought."

And though I fall below it,
I might know as much of mirth
To live and die a poet
Of unacknowledged worth;
For Fame is but a vagrant
Though a loyal one and brave,
And his laurels ne'er so fragrant
As when scattered o'er the grave.

THE OLD-FASHIONED BIBLE
How dear to my heart are the scenes of my childhood
That now but in mem'ry I sadly review;
The old meeting-house at the edge of the wildwood,
The rail fence, and horses all tethered thereto;
The low, sloping roof, and the bell in the steeple,
The doves that came fluttering out overhead
As it solemnly gathered the God-fearing people
To hear the old Bible my grandfather read.
The old-fashioned Bible
The dust-covered Bible
The leathern-bound Bible my grandfather read.

The blessed old volume! The face bent above it
As now I recall it is gravely severe,
Though the reverent eye that droops downward to love it
Makes grander the text through the lens of a tear,
And, as down his features it trickles and glistens,
The cough of the deacon is stilled, and his head
Like a haloed patriarch's leans as he listens
To hear the old Bible my grandfather read.
The old-fashioned Bible
The dust-covered Bible
The leathern-bound Bible my grandfather read.

Ah! who shall look backward with scorn and derision
And scoff the old book though it uselessly lies
In the dust of the past, while this newer revision
Lisps on of a hope and a home in the skies?

Shall the voice of the Master be stifled and riven?
Shall we hear but a tithe of the words He has said,
When so long He has, listening, leaned out of Heaven
To hear the old Bible my grandfather read?
The old-fashioned Bible
The dust-covered Bible
The leathern-bound Bible my grandfather read.

GOOD-BY ER HOWDY-DO
Say good-by er howdy-do
What's the odds betwixt the two?
Comin' goin', ev'ry day
Best friends first to go away
Grasp of hands you'd ruther hold
Than their weight in solid gold
Slips their grip while greetin' you.
Say good-by er howdy-do!

Howdy-do, and then, good-by
Mixes jes' like laugh and cry;
Deaths and births, and worst and best,
Tangled their contrariest;
Ev'ry jinglin' weddin'-bell
Skeerin' up some funer'l knell.
Here's my song, and there's your sigh.
Howdy-do, and then, good-by!

Say good-by er howdy-do
Jes' the same to me and you;
'Taint worth while to make no fuss,
'Cause the job's put up on us!
Some One's runnin' this concern
That's got nothin' else to learn:
Ef He's willin', we'll pull through
Say good-by er howdy-do!

WHEN WE THREE MEET
When we three meet? Ah! friend of mine
Whose verses well and flow as wine,
My thirsting fancy thou dost fill
With draughts delicious, sweeter still
Since tasted by those lips of thine.

I pledge thee, through the chill sunshine
Of autumn, with a warmth divine,
Thrilled through as only I shall thrill
When we three meet.

I pledge thee, if we fast or dine,
We yet shall loosen, line by line,
Old ballads, and the blither trill
Of our-time singers for there will
Be with us all the Muses nine
When we three meet.

"THE LITTLE MAN IN THE TINSHOP"
When I was a little boy, long ago,
And spoke of the theater as the "show,"
The first one that I went to see,
Mother's brother it was took me
(My uncle, of course, though he seemed to be
Only a boy I loved him so!)
And ah, how pleasant he made it all!
And the things he knew that I should know!
The stage, the "drop," and the frescoed wall;
The sudden flash of the lights; and oh,
The orchestra, with its melody,
And the lilt and jingle and jubilee
Of "The Little Man in the Tinshop"!

For Uncle showed me the "Leader" there,
With his pale, bleak forehead and long, black hair;
Showed me the "Second," and "'Cello," and "Bass,"
And the "B-Flat," pouting and puffing his face
At the little end of the horn he blew
Silvery bubbles of music through;
And he coined me names of them, each in turn,
Some comical name that I laughed to learn,
Clean on down to the last and best,
The lively little man, never at rest,
Who hides away at the end of the string,
And tinkers and plays on everything,
That's "The Little Man in the Tinshop"!

Raking a drum like a rattle of hail,
Clinking a cymbal or castanet;
Chirping a twitter or sending a wail
Through a piccolo that thrills me yet;
Reeling ripples of riotous bells,
And tipsy tinkles of triangles
Wrangled and tangled in skeins of sound
Till it seemed that my very soul spun round,
As I leaned, in a breathless joy, toward my
Radiant uncle, who snapped his eye
And said, with the courtliest wave of his hand,
"Why, that little master of all the band

Is 'The Little Man in the Tinshop'!

"And I've heard Verdi, the Wonderful,
And Paganini, and Ole Bull,
Mozart, Handel, and Mendelssohn,
And fair Parepa, whose matchless tone
Karl, her master, with magic bow,
Blent with the angels', and held her so
Tranced till the rapturous Infinite
And I've heard arias, faint and low,
From many an operatic light
Glimmering on my swimming sight
Dimmer and dimmer, until, at last,
I still sit, holding my roses fast
For 'The Little Man in the Tinshop.'"

Oho! my Little Man, joy to you
And yours and theirs your lifetime through!
Though I've heard melodies, boy and man,
Since first "the show" of my life began,
Never yet have I listened to
Sadder, madder, or gladder glees
Than your unharmonied harmonies;
For yours is the music that appeals
To all the fervor the boy's heart feels
All his glories, his wildest cheers,
His bravest hopes, and his brightest tears;
And so, with his first bouquet, he kneels
To "The Little Man in the Tinshop."

TOMMY SMITH

Dimple-cheeked and rosy-lipped,
With his cap-rim backward tipped,
Still in fancy I can see
Little Tommy smile on me
Little Tommy Smith.

Little unsung Tommy Smith
Scarce a name to rhyme it with;
Yet most tenderly to me
Something sings unceasingly
Little Tommy Smith.

On the verge of some far land
Still forever does he stand,
With his cap-rim rakishly
Tilted; so he smiles on me
Little Tommy Smith.

Elder-blooms contrast the grace
Of the rover's radiant face
Whistling back, in mimicry,
"Old Bob White!" all liquidly
Little Tommy Smith.

O my jaunty statuette
Of first love, I see you yet.
Though you smile so mistily,
It is but through tears I see,
Little Tommy Smith.

But, with crown tipped back behind,
And the glad hand of the wind
Smoothing back your hair, I see
Heaven's best angel smile on me,
Little Tommy Smith.

TOM VAN ARDEN

Tom Van Arden, my old friend,
Our warm fellowship is one
Far too old to comprehend
Where its bond was first begun:
Mirage-like before my gaze
Gleams a land of other days,
Where two truant boys, astray,
Dream their lazy lives away.

There's a vision, in the guise
Of Midsummer, where the Past
Like a weary beggar lies
In the shadow Time has cast;
And as blends the bloom of trees
With the drowsy hum of bees,
Fragrant thoughts and murmurs blend,
Tom Van Arden, my old friend.

Tom Van Arden, my old friend,
All the pleasures we have known
Thrill me now as I extend
This old hand and grasp your own
Feeling, in the rude caress,
All affection's tenderness;
Feeling, though the touch be rough,
Our old souls are soft enough.

So we'll make a mellow hour:
Fill your pipe, and taste the wine
Warp your face, if it be sour,

I can spare a smile from mine;
If it sharpen up your wit,
Let me feel the edge of it
I have eager ears to lend,
Tom Van Arden, my old friend.

Tom Van Arden, my old friend,
Are we "lucky dogs," indeed?
Are we all that we pretend
In the jolly life we lead?
Bachelors, we must confess,
Boast of "single blessedness"
To the world, but not alone
Man's best sorrow is his own!

And the saddest truth is this,
Life to us has never proved
What we tasted in the kiss
Of the women we have loved:
Vainly we congratulate
Our escape from such a fate
As their lying lips could send,
Tom Van Arden, my old friend!

Tom Van Arden, my old friend,
Hearts, like fruit upon the stem,
Ripen sweetest, I contend,
As the frost falls over them:
Your regard for me to-day
Makes November taste of May,
And through every vein of rhyme
Pours the blood of summer-time.

When our souls are cramped with youth
Happiness seems far away
In the future, while, in truth,
We look back on it to-day
Through our tears, nor dare to boast,
"Better to have loved and lost!"
Broken hearts are hard to mend,
Tom Van Arden, my old friend.

Tom Van Arden, my old friend,
I grow prosy, and you tire;
Fill the glasses while I bend
To prod up the failing fire. . . .
You are restless: I presume
There's a dampness in the room.
Much of warmth our nature begs,
With rheumatics in our legs! . . .

Humph! the legs we used to fling
Limber-jointed in the dance,
When we heard the fiddle ring
Up the curtain of Romance,
And in crowded public halls
Played with hearts like jugglers' balls.
Feats of mountebanks, depend!
Tom Van Arden, my old friend.

Tom Van Arden, my old friend,
Pardon, then, this theme of mine:
While the firelight leaps to lend
Higher color to the wine,
I propose a health to those
Who have homes, and home's repose,
Wife- and child-love without end!
. . . Tom Van Arden, my old friend.

OUR OLD FRIEND NEVERFAIL

O it's good to ketch a relative 'at's richer and don't run
When you holler out to hold up, and'll joke and have his fun;
It's good to hear a man called bad and then find out he's not,
Er strike some chap they call lukewarm 'at's really red-hot;

It's good to know the Devil's painted jes' a leetle black,
And it's good to have most anybody pat you on the back;
But jes' the best thing in the world's our old friend Neverfail,
When he wags yer hand as honest as an old dog wags his tail!

I like to strike the man I owe the same time I can pay,
And take back things I've borried, and su'prise folks thataway;
I like to find out that the man I voted fer last fall,
That didn't git elected, was a scoundrel after all;
I like the man that likes the pore and he'ps 'em when he can;
I like to meet a ragged tramp 'at's still a gentleman;
But most I like with you, my boy our old friend Neverfail,
When he wags yer hand as honest as an old dog wags his tail!

MY BACHELOR CHUM

A corpulent man is my bachelor chum,
With a neck apoplectic and thick
An abdomen on him as big as a drum,
And a fist big enough for the stick;
With a walk that for grace is clear out of the case,
And a wobble uncertain as though
His little bow-legs had forgotten the pace
That in youth used to favor him so.

He is forty, at least; and the top of his head
Is a bald and a glittering thing;
And his nose and his two chubby cheeks are as red
As three rival roses in spring;

His mouth is a grin with the corners tucked in,
And his laugh is so breezy and bright
That it ripples his features and dimples his chin
With a billowy look of delight.

He is fond of declaring he "don't care a straw"
That "the ills of a bachelor's life
Are blisses, compared with a mother-in-law
And a boarding-school miss for a wife!"
So he smokes and he drinks, and he jokes and he winks,
And he dines and he wines, all alone,
With a thumb ever ready to snap as he thinks
Of the comforts he never has known.

But up in his den (Ah, my bachelor chum!)
I have sat with him there in the gloom,
When the laugh of his lips died away to become
But a phantom of mirth in the room.
And to look on him there you would love him, for all
His ridiculous ways, and be dumb
As the little girl-face that smiles down from the wall
On the tears of my bachelor chum.

ART AND POETRY - TO HOMER DAVENPORT
Wess he says, and sort o' grins,
"Art and Poetry is twins!

"Yit, if I'd my pick, I'd shake
Poetry, and no mistake!

"Pictures, allus, 'peared to me,
Clean laid over Poetry!

"Let me draw, and then, i jings,
I'll not keer a straw who sings.

"'F I could draw as you have drew,
Like to jes' swop pens with you!

"Picture-drawin' 's my pet vision
Of Life-work in Lands Elysian.

"Pictures is first language we

Find hacked out in History.

"Most delight we ever took
Was in our first Picture-book.

"'Thout the funny picture-makers,
They'd be lots more undertakers!

"Still, as I say, Rhymes and Art
'Smighty hard to tell apart.

"Songs and pictures go together
Same as birds and summer weather."

So Wess says, and sort o' grins,
"Art and Poetry is twins."

DOWN TO THE CAPITAL

I' be'n down to the Capital at Washington, D. C.,
Where Congerss meets and passes on the pensions ort to be
Allowed to old one-legged chaps, like me, 'at sence the war
Don't wear their pants in pairs at all and yit how proud we are!

Old Flukens, from our deestrick, jes' turned in and tuck and made
Me stay with him whilse I was there; and longer 'at I stayed
The more I kep' a-wantin' jes' to kind o' git away,
And yit a-feelin' sociabler with Flukens ever' day.

You see I'd got the idy and I guess most folks agrees
'At men as rich as him, you know, kin do jes' what they please;
A man worth stacks o' money, and a Congerssman and all,
And livin' in a buildin' bigger'n Masonic Hall!

Now mind, I'm not a-faultin' Fluke he made his money square:
We both was Forty-niners, and both bu'sted gittin' there;
I weakened and onwindlassed, and he stuck and stayed and made
His millions; don't know what I'm worth untel my pension's paid.

But I was goin' to tell you er a-ruther goin' to try
To tell you how he's livin' now: gas burnin' mighty nigh
In ever' room about the house; and ever' night, about,
Some blame reception goin' on, and money goin' out.

They's people there from all the world jes' ever' kind 'at lives,
Injuns and all! and Senators, and Ripresentatives;
And girls, you know, jes' dressed in gauze and roses, I declare,
And even old men shamblin' round a-waltzin' with 'em there!

And bands a-tootin' circus-tunes, 'way in some other room

Jes' chokin' full o' hothouse plants and pinies and perfume;
And fountains, squirtin' stiddy all the time; and statutes, made
Out o' puore marble, 'peared-like, sneakin' round there in the shade.

And Fluke he coaxed and begged and pled with me to take a hand
And sashay in amongst 'em crutch and all, you understand;
But when I said how tired I was, and made fer open air,
He follered, and tel five o'clock we set a-talkin' there.

"My God!" says he, Fluke says to me, "I'm tireder'n you!
Don't putt up yer tobacker tel you give a man a chew.
Set back a leetle furder in the shadder that'll do;
I'm tireder'n you, old man; I'm tireder'n you.

"You see that-air old dome," says he, "humped up ag'inst the sky?
It's grand, first time you see it; but it changes, by and by,
And then it stays jes' thataway jes' anchored high and dry
Betwixt the sky up yender and the achin' of yer eye.

"Night's purty; not so purty, though, as what it ust to be
When my first wife was livin'. You remember her?" says he.
I nodded-like, and Fluke went on, "I wonder now ef she
Knows where I am and what I am and what I ust to be?

"That band in there! I ust to think 'at music couldn't wear
A feller out the way it does; but that ain't music there
That's jes' a' imitation, and like ever'thing, I swear,
I hear, er see, er tetch, er taste, er tackle anywhere!

"It's all jes' artificial, this-'ere high-priced life of ours;
The theory, it's sweet enough, tel it saps down and sours.
They's no home left, ner ties o' home about it. By the powers,
The whole thing's artificialer'n artificial flowers!

"And all I want, and could lay down and sob fer, is to know
The homely things of homely life; fer instance, jes' to go
And set down by the kitchen stove, Lord! that 'u'd rest me so,
Jes' set there, like I ust to do, and laugh and joke, you know.

"Jes' set there, like I ust to do," says Fluke, a-startin' in,
'Peared-like, to say the whole thing over to hisse't ag'in;
Then stopped and turned, and kind o' coughed, and stooped and fumbled fer
Somepin' o' 'nuther in the grass, I guess his handkercher.

Well, sence I'm back from Washington, where I left Fluke a-still
A-leggin' fer me, heart and soul, on that-air pension bill,
I've half-way struck the notion, when I think o' wealth and sich,
They's nothin' much patheticker'n jes' a-bein' rich!

OLD CHUMS

"If I die first," my old chum paused to say,
"Mind! not a whimper of regret: instead,
Laugh and be glad, as I shall. Being dead,
I shall not lodge so very far away
But that our mirth shall mingle. So, the day
The word comes, joy with me." "I'll try," I said,
Though, even speaking, sighed and shook my head
And turned, with misted eyes. His roundelay
Rang gaily on the stair; and then the door
Opened and closed. . . . Yet something of the clear,
Hale hope, and force of wholesome faith he had
Abided with me, strengthened more and more.
Then, then they brought his broken body here:
And I laughed, whisperingly and we were glad.

SCOTTY

Scotty's dead. Of course he is!
Jes' that same old luck of his!
Ever sence we went cahoots
He's be'n first, you bet yer boots!
When our schoolin' first begun,
Got two whippin's to my one:
Stold and smoked the first cigar:
Stood up first before the bar,
Takin' whisky-straight and me
Wastin' time on "blackberry"!

Beat me in the Army, too,
And clean on the whole way through!
In more scrapes around the camp,
And more troubles, on the tramp:
Fought and fell there by my side
With more bullets in his hide,
And more glory in the cause,
That's the kind o' man he was!
Luck liked Scotty more'n me.
I got married: Scotty, he
Never even would apply
Fer the pension-money I
Had to beg of "Uncle Sam"
That's the kind o' cuss I am!
Scotty allus first and best
Me the last and ornriest!
Yit fer all that's said and done
All the battles fought and won
We hain't prospered, him ner me
Both as pore as pore could be,
Though we've allus, up tel now,

Stuck together anyhow
Scotty allus, as I've said,
Luckiest, And now he's dead!

THE OLD MAN

Lo! steadfast and serene,
In patient pause between
The seen and the unseen,
What gentle zephyrs fan
Your silken silver hair,
And what diviner air
Breathes round you like a prayer,
Old Man?

Can you, in nearer view
Of Glory, pierce the blue
Of happy Heaven through;
And, listening mutely, can
Your senses, dull to us,
Hear Angel-voices thus,
In chorus glorious
Old Man?

In your reposeful gaze
The dusk of Autumn days
Is blent with April haze,
As when of old began
The bursting of the bud
Of rosy babyhood
When all the world was good,
Old Man.

And yet I find a sly
Little twinkle in your eye;
And your whisperingly shy
Little laugh is simply an
Internal shout of glee
That betrays the fallacy
You'd perpetrate on me,
Old Man.

So just put up the frown
That your brows are pulling down!
Why, the fleetest boy in town,
As he bared his feet and ran,
Could read with half a glance
And of keen rebuke, perchance
Your secret countenance,
Old Man.

Now, honestly, confess:
Is an old man any less
Than the little child we bless
And caress when we can?
Isn't age but just a place
Where you mask the childish face
To preserve its inner grace,
Old Man?

Hasn't age a truant day,
Just as that you went astray
In the wayward, restless way,
When, brown with dust and tan,
Your roguish face essayed,
In solemn masquerade,
To hide the smile it made,
Old Man?

Now, fair, and square, and true,
Don't your old soul tremble through,
As in youth it used to do
When it brimmed and overran
With the strange, enchanted sights,
And the splendors and delights
Of the old "Arabian Nights,"
Old Man?

When, haply, you have fared
Where glad Aladdin shared
His lamp with you, and dared
The Afrite and his clan;
And, with him, clambered through
The trees where jewels grew
And filled your pockets, too,
Old Man?

Or, with Sinbad, at sea
And in veracity
Who has sinned as bad as he,
Or would, or will, or can?
Have you listened to his lies,
With open mouth and eyes,
And learned his art likewise,
Old Man?

And you need not deny
That your eyes were wet as dry,
Reading novels on the sly!
And review them, if you can
And the same warm tears will fall

Only faster, that is all
Over Little Nell and Paul,
Old Man!

Oh, you were a lucky lad
Just as good as you were bad!
And the host of friends you had
Charley, Tom, and Dick, and Dan;
And the old School-Teacher, too,
Though he often censured you;
And the girls in pink and blue,
Old Man.

And as often you have leant,
In boyish sentiment,
To kiss the letter sent
By Nelly, Belle, or Nan
Wherein the rose's hue
Was red, the violet blue
And sugar sweet and you,
Old Man,

So, to-day, as lives the bloom,
And the sweetness, and perfume
Of the blossoms, I assume,
On the same mysterious plan
The Master's love assures,
That the selfsame boy endures
In that hale old heart of yours,
Old Man.

JAMES B. MAYNARD
His daily, nightly task is o'er
He leans above his desk no more.

His pencil and his pen say not
One further word of gracious thought.

All silent is his voice, yet clear
For all a grateful world to hear;

He poured abroad his human love
In opulence unmeasured of

While, in return, his meek demand,
The warm clasp of a neighbor-hand

In recognition of the true
World's duty that he lived to do.

So was he kin of yours and mine
So, even by the hallowed sign

Of silence which he listens to,
He hears our tears as falls the dew.

THE ANCIENT PRINTERMAN
O Printerman of sallow face,
And look of absent guile,
Is it the 'copy' on your 'case'
That causes you to smile?
Or is it some old treasure scrap
You call from Memory's file?

"I fain would guess its mystery
For often I can trace
A fellow dreamer's history
Whene'er it haunts the face;
Your fancy's running riot
In a retrospective race!

"Ah, Printerman, you're straying
Afar from 'stick' and type
Your heart has 'gone a-maying,'
And you taste old kisses, ripe
Again on lips that pucker
At your old asthmatic pipe!

"You are dreaming of old pleasures
That have faded from your view;
And the music-burdened measures
Of the laughs you listen to
Are now but angel-echoes
O, have I spoken true?"

The ancient Printer hinted
With a motion full of grace
To where the words were printed
On a card above his "case,"
"'I am deaf and dumb!" I left him
With a smile upon his face.

THE OLD MAN AND JIM
Old man never had much to say
'Ceptin' to Jim,
And Jim was the wildest boy he had

And the old man jes' wrapped up in him!
Never heerd him speak but once
Er twice in my life, and first time was
When the army broke out, and Jim he went,
The old man backin' him, fer three months;
And all 'at I heerd the old man say
Was, jes' as we turned to start away,
"Well, good-by, Jim:
Take keer o' yourse'f!"

'Peared-like, he was more satisfied
Jes' lookin' at Jim
And likin' him all to hisse'f-like, see?
'Cause he was jes' wrapped up in him!
And over and over I mind the day
The old man come and stood round in the way
While we was drillin', a-watchin' Jim
And down at the deepo a-heerin' him say,
"Well, good-by, Jim:
Take keer of yourse'f!"

Never was nothin' about the farm
Disting'ished Jim;
Neighbors all ust to wonder why
The old man 'peared wrapped up in him;
But when Cap. Biggler he writ back
'At Jim was the bravest boy we had
In the whole dern rigiment, white er black,
And his fightin' good as his farmin' bad
'At he had led, with a bullet clean
Bored through his thigh, and carried the flag
Through the bloodiest battle you ever seen,
The old man wound up a letter to him
'At Cap. read to us, 'at said: "Tell Jim
Good-by,
And take keer of hisse'f."

Jim come home jes' long enough
To take the whim
'At he'd like to go back in the calvery
And the old man jes' wrapped up in him!
Jim 'lowed 'at he'd had sich luck afore,
Guessed he'd tackle her three years more.
And the old man give him a colt he'd raised,
And follered him over to Camp Ben Wade,
And laid around fer a week er so,
Watchin' Jim on dress-parade
Tel finally he rid away,
And last he heerd was the old man say,
"Well, good-by, Jim:
Take keer of yourse'f!"

Tuk the papers, the old man did,
A-watchin' fer Jim
Fully believin' he'd make his mark
Some way jes' wrapped up in him!
And many a time the word 'u'd come
'At stirred him up like the tap of a drum
At Petersburg, fer instunce, where
Jim rid right into their cannons there,
And tuk 'em, and p'inted 'em t'other way,
And socked it home to the boys in gray
As they scooted fer timber, and on and on
Jim a lieutenant, and one arm gone,
And the old man's words in his mind all day,
"Well, good-by, Jim:
Take keer of yourse'f!"

Think of a private, now, perhaps,
We'll say like Jim,
'At's dumb clean up to the shoulder-straps
And the old man jes' wrapped up in him!
Think of him with the war plum' through,
And the glorious old Red-White-and-Blue
A-laughin' the news down over Jim,
And the old man, bendin' over him
The surgeon turnin' away with tears
'At hadn't leaked fer years and years,
As the hand of the dyin' boy clung to
His father's, the old voice in his ears,
"Well, good-by, Jim:
Take keer of yourse'f!"

THE OLD SCHOOL-CHUM
He puts the poem by, to say
His eyes are not themselves to-day!

A sudden glamour o'er his sight
A something vague, indefinite

An oft-recurring blur that blinds
The printed meaning of the lines,

And leaves the mind all dusk and dim
In swimming darkness strange to him!

It is not childishness, I guess,
Yet something of the tenderness

That used to wet his lashes when

A boy seems troubling him again;

The old emotion, sweet and wild,
That drove him truant when a child,

That he might hide the tears that fell
Above the lesson "Little Nell."

And so it is he puts aside
The poem he has vainly tried

To follow; and, as one who sighs
In failure, through a poor disguise

Of smiles, he dries his tears,to say
His eyes are not themselves to-day.

MY JOLLY FRIEND'S SECRET
Ah, friend of mine, how goes it
Since you've taken you a mate?
Your smile, though, plainly shows it
Is a very happy state!
Dan Cupid's necromancy!
You must sit you down and dine,
And lubricate your fancy
With a glass or two of wine.

And as you have "deserted,"
As my other chums have done,
While I laugh alone diverted,
As you drop off one by one
And I've remained unwedded,
Till you see look here that I'm,
In a manner, "snatched bald-headed"
By the sportive hand of Time!

I'm an "old 'un!" yes, but wrinkles
Are not so plenty, quite,
As to cover up the twinkles
Of the boy ain't I right?
Yet there are ghosts of kisses
Under this mustache of mine
My mem'ry only misses
When I drown 'em out with wine.

From acknowledgment so ample,
You would hardly take me for
What I am a perfect sample
Of a "jolly bachelor";

Not a bachelor has being
When he laughs at married life
But his heart and soul's agreeing
That he ought to have a wife!

Ah, ha! old chum, this claret,
Like Fatima, holds the key
Of the old Blue-Beardish garret
Of my hidden mystery!
Did you say you'd like to listen?
Ah, my boy! the "Sad No More!"
And the tear-drops that will glisten
Turn the catch upon the door,

And sit you down beside me
And put yourself at ease
I'll trouble you to slide me
That wine decanter, please;
The path is kind o' mazy
Where my fancies have to go,
And my heart gets sort o' lazy
On the journey don't you know?

Let me see, when I was twenty
It's a lordly age, my boy,
When a fellow's money's plenty,
And the leisure to enjoy

And a girl, with hair as golden
As that; and lips well quite
As red as this I'm holdin'
Between you and the light?

And eyes and a complexion
Ah, heavens! le'-me-see
Well, just in this connection,
Did you lock that door for me?
Did I start in recitation
My past life to recall?
Well, that's an indication
I am purty tight that's all!

IN THE HEART OF JUNE
In the heart of June, love,
You and I together,
On from dawn till noon, love,
Laughing with the weather;
Blending both our souls, love,
In the selfsame tune,

Drinking all life holds, love,
In the heart of June.

In the heart of June, love,
With its golden weather,
Underneath the moon, love,
You and I together.
Ah! how sweet to seem, love,
Drugged and half aswoon
With this luscious dream, love,
In the heart of June.

THE OLD BAND

It's mighty good to git back to the old town, shore,
Considerin' I've be'n away twenty year and more.
Sence I moved then to Kansas, of course I see a change,
A-comin' back, and notice things that's new to me and strange;
Especially at evening when yer new band-fellers meet,
In fancy uniforms and all, and play out on the street
 . . . What's come of old Bill Lindsey and the Saxhorn fellers say?
I want to hear the old band play.

What's come of Eastman, and Nat Snow? And where's War Barnett at?
And Nate and Bony Meek; Bill Hart; Tom Richa'son and that-
Air brother of him played the drum as twic't as big as Jim;
And old Hi Kerns, the carpenter say, what's become o' him?
I make no doubt yer new band now's a competenter band,
And plays their music more by note than what they play by hand,
And stylisher and grander tunes; but somehow, anyway,
I want to hear the old band play.

Sich tunes as "John Brown's Body" and "Sweet Alice," don't you know;
And "The Camels is A-comin'," and "John Anderson, my Jo";
And a dozent others of 'em "Number Nine" and "Number 'Leven"
Was favo-rites that fairly made a feller dream o' Heaven.
And when the boys 'u'd saranade, I've laid so still in bed
I've even heerd the locus'-blossoms droppin' on the shed
When "Lilly Dale," er "Hazel Dell," had sobbed and died away
 . . . I want to hear the old band play.

Yer new band ma'by beats it, but the old band's what I said
It allus 'peared to kind o' chord with somepin' in my head;
And, whilse I'm no musicianer, when my blame' eyes is jes'
Nigh drownded out, and Mem'ry squares her jaws and sort o' says
She won't ner never will fergit, I want to jes' turn in
And take and light right out o' here and git back West ag'in
And stay there, when I git there, where I never haf to say
I want to hear the old band play.

MY FRIEND

"He is my friend," I said,
"Be patient!" Overhead
The skies were drear and dim;
And lo! the thought of him
Smiled on my heart and then
The sun shone out again!

"He is my friend!" The words
Brought summer and the birds;
And all my winter-time
Thawed into running rhyme
And rippled into song,
Warm, tender, brave, and strong.

And so it sings to-day.
So may it sing alway!
Though waving grasses grow
Between, and lilies blow
Their trills of perfume clear
As laughter to the ear,
Let each mute measure end
With "Still he is thy friend."

THE TRAVELING MAN

I

Could I pour out the nectar the gods only can,
I would fill up my glass to the brim
And drink the success of the Traveling Man,
And the house represented by him;
And could I but tincture the glorious draught
With his smiles, as I drank to him then,
And the jokes he has told and the laughs he has laughed,
I would fill up the goblet again

And drink to the sweetheart who gave him good-by
With a tenderness thrilling him this
Very hour, as he thinks of the tear in her eye
That salted the sweet of her kiss;
To her truest of hearts and her fairest of hands
I would drink, with all serious prayers,
Since the heart she must trust is a Traveling Man's,
And as warm as the ulster he wears.

II

I would drink to the wife, with the babe on her knee,
Who awaits his returning in vain

Who breaks his brave letters so tremulously
And reads them again and again!
And I'd drink to the feeble old mother who sits
At the warm fireside of her son
And murmurs and weeps o'er the stocking she knits,
As she thinks of the wandering one.

I would drink a long life and a health to the friends
Who have met him with smiles and with cheer
To the generous hand that the landlord extends
To the wayfarer journeying here:
And I pledge, when he turns from this earthly abode
And pays the last fare that he can,
Mine Host of the Inn at the End of the Road
Will welcome the Traveling Man!

DAN O'SULLIVAN

Dan O'Sullivan: It's your
Lips have kissed "The Blarney," sure!
To be trillin' praise av me,
Dhrippin' swhate wid poethry!
Not that I'd not have ye sing
Don't lave off for anything
Jusht be aisy whilst the fit
Av me head shwells up to it!

Dade and thrue, I'm not the man,
Whilst yer singin', loike ye can,
To cry shtop because ye've blesht
My songs more than all the resht:
I'll not be the b'y to ax
Any shtar to wane or wax,
Or ax any clock that's woun'
To run up inshtid av down!

Whist yez! Dan O'Sullivan!
Him that made the Irishman
Mixt the birds in wid the dough,
And the dew and mistletoe
Wid the whusky in the quare
Muggs av us and here we air,
Three parts right, and three parts wrong,
Shpiked with beauty, wit and song!

MY OLD FRIEND

You've a manner all so mellow,
My old friend,

That it cheers and warms a fellow,
My old friend,
Just to meet and greet you, and
Feel the pressure of a hand
That one may understand,
My old friend.

Though dimmed in youthful splendor,
My old friend,
Your smiles are still as tender,
My old friend,
And your eyes as true a blue
As your childhood ever knew,
And your laugh as merry, too,
My old friend.

For though your hair is faded,
My old friend,
And your step a trifle jaded,
My old friend,
Old Time, with all his lures
In the trophies he secures,
Leaves young that heart of yours,
My old friend.

And so it is you cheer me,
My old friend,
For to know you still are near me,
My old friend,
Makes my hopes of clearer light,
And my faith of surer sight,
And my soul a purer white,
My old friend.

OLD JOHN HENRY

Old John's jes' made o' the commonest stuff
Old John Henry
He's tough, I reckon, but none too tough
Too tough though's better than not enough!
Says old John Henry.
He does his best, and when his best's bad,
He don't fret none, ner he don't git sad
He simply 'lows it's the best he had:
Old John Henry!

His doctern's jes' o' the plainest brand
Old John Henry
A smilin' face and a hearty hand
'S religen 'at all folks understand,

Says old John Henry.
He's stove up some with the rhumatiz,
And they hain't no shine on them shoes o' his,
And his hair hain't cut but his eye-teeth is:
Old John Henry!

He feeds hisse'f when the stock's all fed
Old John Henry
And sleeps like a babe when he goes to bed
And dreams o' Heaven and home-made bread,
Says old John Henry.
He hain't refined as he'd ort to be
To fit the statutes o' poetry,
Ner his clothes don't fit him but he fits me:
Old John Henry!

HER VALENTINE

Somebody's sent a funny little valentine to me.
It's a bunch of baby-roses in a vase of filigree,
And hovering above them just as cute as he can be
Is a fairy Cupid tangled in a scarf of poetry.

And the prankish little fellow looks so knowing in his glee,
With his golden bow and arrow, aiming most unerringly
At a pair of hearts so labeled that I may read and see
That one is meant for "One Who Loves," and one is meant for me.

But I know the lad who sent it! It's as plain as A-B-C!
For the roses they are blushing, and the vase stands awkwardly,
And the little god above it though as cute as he can be
Can not breathe the lightest whisper of his burning love for me.

CHRISTMAS GREETING

A word of Godspeed and good cheer
To all on earth, or far or near,
Or friend or foe, or thine or mine
In echo of the voice divine,
Heard when the star bloomed forth and lit
The world's face, with God's smile on it.

ABE MARTIN

Abe Martin! dad-burn his old picture!
P'tends he's a Brown County fixture
A kind of a comical mixture
Of hoss-sense and no sense at all!

His mouth, like his pipe, 's allus goin',
And his thoughts, like his whiskers, is flowin',
And what he don't know ain't wuth knowin'
From Genesis clean to baseball!

The artist, Kin Hubbard, 's so keerless
He draws Abe 'most eyeless and earless,
But he's never yet pictured him cheerless
Er with fun 'at he tries to conceal,
Whuther on to the fence er clean over
A-rootin' up ragweed er clover,
Skeert stiff at some "Rambler" er "Rover"
Er newfangled automobeel!

It's a purty steep climate old Brown's in;
And the rains there his ducks nearly drowns in
The old man hisse'f wades his rounds in
As ca'm and serene, mighty nigh
As the old handsaw-hawg, er the mottled
Milch cow, er the old rooster wattled
Like the mumps had him 'most so well throttled
That it was a pleasure to die.

But best of 'em all's the fool-breaks 'at
Abe don't see at all, and yit makes 'at
Both me and you lays back and shakes at
His comic, miraculous cracks
Which makes him clean back of the power
Of genius itse'f in its flower
This Notable Man of the Hour,
Abe Martin, The Joker on Facts.

THE LITTLE OLD POEM THAT NOBODY READS

The little old poem that nobody reads
Blooms in a crowded space,
Like a ground-vine blossom, so low in the weeds
That nobody sees its face
Unless, perchance, the reader's eye
Stares through a yawn, and hurries by,
For no one wants, or loves, or heeds,
The little old poem that nobody reads.

The little old poem that nobody reads
Was written where? and when?
Maybe a hand of goodly deeds
Thrilled as it held the pen:
Maybe the fountain whence it came
Was a heart brimmed o'er with tears of shame,
And maybe its creed is the worst of creeds

The little old poem that nobody reads.

But, little old poem that nobody reads,
Holding you here above
The wound of a heart that warmly bleeds
For all that knows not love,
I well believe if the old World knew
As dear a friend as I find in you,
That friend would tell it that all it needs
Is the little old poem that nobody reads.

IN THE AFTERNOON

You in the hammock; and I, near by,
Was trying to read, and to swing you, too;
And the green of the sward was so kind to the eye,
And the shade of the maples so cool and blue,
That often I looked from the book to you
To say as much, with a sigh.

You in the hammock. The book we'd brought
From the parlor to read in the open air,
Something of love and of Launcelot
And Guinevere, I believe, was there
But the afternoon, it was far more fair
Than the poem was, I thought.

You in the hammock; and on and on.
I droned and droned through the rhythmic stuff
But, with always a half of my vision gone
Over the top of the page enough
To caressingly gaze at you, swathed in the fluff
Of your hair and your odorous "lawn."

You in the hammock and that was a year
Fully a year ago, I guess
And what do we care for their Guinevere
And her Launcelot and their lordliness!
You in the hammock still, and Yes
Kiss me again, my dear!

BECAUSE

Why did we meet long years of yore?
And why did we strike hands and say
"We will be friends and nothing more";
Why are we musing thus to-day?
Because because was just because,
And no one knew just why it was.

Why did I say good-by to you?
Why did I sail across the main?
Why did I love not heaven's own blue
Until I touched these shores again?
Because because was just because,
And you nor I knew why it was.

Why are my arms about you now,
And happy tears upon your cheek?
And why my kisses on your brow?
Look up in thankfulness and speak!
Because because was just because,
And only God knew why it was.

HERR WEISER

Herr Weiser! Threescore years and ten,
A hale white rose of his countrymen,
Transplanted here in the Hoosier loam,
And blossomy as his German home
As blossomy and as pure and sweet
As the cool green glen of his calm retreat,
Far withdrawn from the noisy town
Where trade goes clamoring up and down,
Whose fret and fever, and stress and strife,
May not trouble his tranquil life!

Breath of rest, what a balmy gust!
Quit of the city's heat and dust,
Jostling down by the winding road
Through the orchard ways of his quaint abode.
Tether the horse, as we onward fare
Under the pear trees trailing there,
And thumping the wooden bridge at night
With lumps of ripeness and lush delight,
Till the stream, as it maunders on till dawn,
Is powdered and pelted and smiled upon.

Herr Weiser, with his wholesome face,
And the gentle blue of his eyes, and grace
Of unassuming honesty,
Be there to welcome you and me!
And what though the toil of the farm be stopped
And the tireless plans of the place be dropped,
While the prayerful master's knees are set
In beds of pansy and mignonette
And lily and aster and columbine,
Offered in love, as yours and mine?

What, but a blessing of kindly thought,
Sweet as the breath of forget-me-not!
What, but a spirit of lustrous love
White as the aster he bends above!
What, but an odorous memory
Of the dear old man, made known to me
In days demanding a help like his,
As sweet as the life of the lily is
As sweet as the soul of a babe, bloom-wise
Born of a lily in Paradise.

A MOTHER-SONG

Mother, O mother! forever I cry for you,
Sing the old song I may never forget;
Even in slumber I murmur and sigh for you.
Mother, O mother,
Sing low, "Little brother,
Sleep, for thy mother bends over thee yet!"

Mother, O mother! the years are so lonely,
Filled but with weariness, doubt and regret!
Can't you come back to me for to-night only,
Mother, my mother,
And sing, "Little brother,
Sleep, for thy mother bends over thee yet!"

Mother, O mother! of old I had never
One wish denied me, nor trouble to fret;
Now must I cry out all vainly forever,
Mother, sweet mother,
O sing, "Little brother,
Sleep, for thy mother bends over thee yet!"

Mother, O mother! must longing and sorrow
Leave me in darkness, with eyes ever wet,
And never the hope of a meeting to-morrow?
Answer me, mother,
And sing, "Little brother,
Sleep, for thy mother bends over thee yet!"

WHAT "OLD SANTA" OVERHEARD

'Tis said old Santa Claus one time
Told this joke on himself in rhyme:
One Christmas, in the early din
That ever leads the morning in,
I heard the happy children shout
In rapture at the toys turned out

Of bulging little socks and shoes
A joy at which I could but choose
To listen enviously, because
I'm always just "Old Santa Claus,"
But ere my rising sigh had got
To its first quaver at the thought,
It broke in laughter, as I heard
A little voice chirp like a bird,

"Old Santa's mighty good, I know.
And awful rich and he can go
Down ever' chimbly anywhere
In all the world! But I don't care,
I wouldn't trade with him, and be
Old Santa Clause, and him be me,
Fer all his toys and things! and I
Know why, and bet you he knows why!
They wuz no Santa Clause when he
Wuz ist a little boy like me!"

THE STEPMOTHER

First she come to our house,
Tommy run and hid;
And Emily and Bob and me
We cried jus' like we did
When Mother died, and we all said
'At we all wisht 'at we was dead!

And Nurse she couldn't stop us;
And Pa he tried and tried,
We sobbed and shook and wouldn't look,
But only cried and cried;
And nen some one we couldn't jus'
Tell who was cryin' same as us!

Our Stepmother! Yes, it was her,
Her arms around us all
'Cause Tom slid down the banister
And peeked in from the hall.
And we all love her, too, because
She's purt' nigh good as Mother was!

WHEN OLD JACK DIED

When Old Jack died, we stayed from school (they said,
At home, we needn't go that day), and none
Of us ate any breakfast only one,
And that was Papa and his eyes were red

When he came round where we were, by the shed
Where Jack was lying, half-way in the sun
And half-way in the shade. When we begun
To cry out loud, Pa turned and dropped his head
And went away; and Mamma, she went back
Into the kitchen. Then, for a long while,
All to ourselves, like, we stood there and cried.
We thought so many good things of Old Jack,
And funny things although we didn't smile
We couldn't only cry when Old Jack died.

When Old Jack died, it seemed a human friend
Had suddenly gone from us; that some face
That we had loved to fondle and embrace
From babyhood, no more would condescend
To smile on us forever. We might bend
With tearful eyes above him, interlace
Our chubby fingers o'er him, romp and race,
Plead with him, call and coax aye, we might send
The old halloo up for him, whistle, hist,
(If sobs had let us) or, as wildly vain,
Snapped thumbs, called "Speak," and he had not replied;
We might have gone down on our knees and kissed
The tousled ears, and yet they must remain
Deaf, motionless, we knew when Old Jack died.

When Old Jack died, it seemed to us, some way,
That all the other dogs in town were pained
With our bereavement, and some that were chained,
Even, unslipped their collars on that day
To visit Jack in state, as though to pay
A last, sad tribute there, while neighbors craned
Their heads above the high board fence, and deigned
To sigh "Poor Dog!" remembering how they
Had cuffed him, when alive, perchance, because,
For love of them he leaped to lick their hands
Now, that he could not, were they satisfied?
We children thought that, as we crossed his paws,
And o'er his grave, 'way down the bottom-lands,
Wrote "Our First Love Lies Here," when Old Jack died.

THAT NIGHT

You and I, and that night, with its perfume and glory!
The scent of the locusts the light of the moon;
And the violin weaving the waltzers a story,
Enmeshing their feet in the weft of the tune,
Till their shadows uncertain
Reeled round on the curtain,
While under the trellis we drank in the June.

Soaked through with the midnight the cedars were sleeping,
Their shadowy tresses outlined in the bright
Crystal, moon-smitten mists, where the fountain's heart, leaping
Forever, forever burst, full with delight;
And its lisp on my spirit
Fell faint as that near it
Whose love like a lily bloomed out in the night.

O your glove was an odorous sachet of blisses!
The breath of your fan was a breeze from Cathay!
And the rose at your throat was a nest of spilled kisses!
And the music! in fancy I hear it to-day,
As I sit here, confessing
Our secret, and blessing
My rival who found us, and waltzed you away.

TO ALMON KEEFER - INSCRIBED IN "TALES OF THE OCEAN"
This first book that I ever knew
Was read aloud to me by you
Friend of my boyhood, therefore take
It back from me, for old times' sake
The selfsame "Tales" first read to me,
Under "the old sweet apple tree,"
Ere I myself could read such great
Big words, but listening all elate,
At your interpreting, until
Brain, heart and soul were all athrill
With wonder, awe, and sheer excess
Of wildest childish happiness.

So take the book again forget
All else, long years, lost hopes, regret;
Sighs for the joys we ne'er attain,
Prayers we have lifted all in vain;
Tears for the faces seen no more,
Once as the roses at the door!
Take the enchanted book And lo,
On grassy swards of long ago,
Sprawl out again, beneath the shade
The breezy old-home orchard made,
The veriest barefoot boy indeed
And I will listen as you read.

TO THE QUIET OBSERVER - AFTER HIS LONG SILENCE
Dear old friend of us all in need
Who know the worth of a friend indeed,

How rejoiced are we all to learn
Of your glad return.

We who have missed your voice so long
Even as March might miss the song
Of the sugar-bird in the maples when
They're tapped again.

Even as the memory of these
Blended sweets, the sap of the trees
And the song of the birds, and the old camp too,
We think of you.

Hail to you, then, with welcomes deep
As grateful hearts may laugh or weep!
You give us not only the bird that sings,
But all good things.

REACH YOUR HAND TO ME
Reach your hand to me, my friend,
With its heartiest caress
Sometime there will come an end
To its present faithfulness
Sometime I may ask in vain
For the touch of it again,
When between us land or sea
Holds it ever back from me.

Sometime I may need it so,
Groping somewhere in the night,
It will seem to me as though
Just a touch, however light,
Would make all the darkness day,
And along some sunny way
Lead me through an April-shower
Of my tears to this fair hour.

O the present is too sweet
To go on forever thus!
Round the corner of the street
Who can say what waits for us?
Meeting, greeting, night and day,
Faring each the selfsame way
Still somewhere the path must end
Reach your hand to me, my friend!

THE DEAD JOKE AND THE FUNNY MAN

Long years ago, a funny man,
Flushed with a strange delight,
Sat down and wrote a funny thing
All in the solemn night;
And as he wrote he clapped his hands
And laughed with all his might.
For it was such a funny thing,
O, such a very funny thing,
This wonderfully funny thing,
He
Laughed
Outright.

And so it was this funny man
Printed this funny thing
Forgot it, too, nor ever thought
It worth remembering,
Till but a day or two ago.
(Ah! what may changes bring!)
He found this selfsame funny thing
In an exchange "O, funny thing!"
He cried, "You dear old funny thing!"
And
Sobbed
Outright.

AMERICA'S THANKSGIVING - 1900

Father all bountiful, in mercy bear
With this our universal voice of prayer
The voice that needs must be
Upraised in thanks to Thee,
O Father, from Thy children everywhere.

A multitudinous voice, wherein we fain
Wouldst have Thee hear no lightest sob of pain
No murmur of distress,
Nor moan of loneliness,
Nor drip of tears, though soft as summer rain.

And, Father, give us first to comprehend,
No ill can come from Thee; lean Thou and lend
Us clearer sight to see
Our boundless debt to Thee,
Since all Thy deeds are blessings, in the end.

And let us feel and know that, being Thine,
We are inheritors of hearts divine,
And hands endowed with skill,
And strength to work Thy will,

And fashion to fulfilment Thy design.

So, let us thank Thee, with all self aside,
Nor any lingering taint of mortal pride;
As here to Thee we dare
Uplift our faltering prayer,
Lend it some fervor of the glorified.

We thank Thee that our land is loved of Thee
The blessed home of thrift and industry,
With ever-open door
Of welcome to the poor
Thy shielding hand o'er all abidingly.

E'en thus we thank Thee for the wrong that grew
Into a right that heroes battled to,
With brothers long estranged,
Once more as brothers ranged
Beneath the red and white and starry blue.

Ay, thanks though tremulous the thanks expressed
Thanks for the battle at its worst, and best
For all the clanging fray
Whose discord dies away
Into a pastoral-song of peace and rest.

OLD INDIANY - INTENDED FOR A DINNER OF THE INDIANA SOCIETY OF CHICAGO
Old Indiany, 'course we know
Is first, and best, and most, also,
Of all the States' whole forty-four:
She's first in ever'thing, that's shore!
And best in ever'way as yet
Made known to man; and you kin bet
She's most, because she won't confess
She ever was, or will be, less!
And yet, fer all her proud array
Of sons, how many gits away!

No doubt about her bein' great,
But, fellers, she's a leaky State!
And them that boasts the most about
Her, them's the ones that's dribbled out.
Law! jes' to think of all you boys
'Way over here in Illinoise
A-celebratin', like ye air,
Old Indiany, 'way back there
In the dark ages, so to speak,
A-prayin' for ye once a week
And wonderin' what's a-keepin' you

From comin', like you ort to do.
You're all a-lookin' well, and like
You wasn't "sidin' up the pike,"
As the tramp-shoemaker said
When "he sacked the boss and shed
The blame town, to hunt fer one
Where they didn't work fer fun!"
Lookin' extry well, I'd say,
Your old home so fur away.

Maybe, though, like the old jour.,
Fun hain't all yer workin' fer.
So you've found a job that pays
Better than in them old days
You was on The Weekly Press,
Heppin' run things, more er less;
Er a-learnin' telegraph
Operatin', with a half
Notion of the tinner's trade,
Er the dusty man's that laid
Out designs on marble and
Hacked out little lambs by hand,
And chewed finecut as he wrought,
"Shapin' from his bitter thought"
Some squshed mutterings to say,
"Yes, hard work, and porer pay!"
Er you'd kind o' thought the far
Gazin' kuss that owned a car
And took pictures in it, had
Jes' the snap you wanted bad!
And you even wondered why
He kep' foolin' with his sky
Light the same on shiny days
As when rainin'. ('T leaked always.)

Wondered what strange things was hid
In there when he shet the door
And smelt like a burnt drug store
Next some orchard-trees, I swan!
With whole roasted apples on!
That's why Ade is, here of late,
Buyin' in the dear old state,
So's to cut it up in plots
Of both town and country lots.

James Whitcomb Riley – A Short Biography

Poet and author James Whitcomb Riley was born on October 7th 1849 in Greenfield, Indiana. Known as the "Hoosier Poet" for his work with regional dialects, and as the "Children's Poet" for his children's poetry and devotion to youth causes, Riley is best remembered as the author of the well-loved verse book, *Rhymes of Childhood*.

Riley grew up in a well-off and influential family. Riley's father, Reuben Andrew Riley, was a lawyer and Democrat member of the Indiana House of Representatives and he named his son for his friend James Whitcomb, then the governor of Indiana.

Riley had a spotty education, learning at home and attending his local school sporadically (he did not graduate Grade 8 until the age of twenty). Nonetheless, his was a childhood full of creativity. He learned about poetry from an uncle who was a poet and enthusiast and was encouraged by his mother to write and produce juvenile theatrical presentations. His father taught him how to play the guitar and Riley went on to perform in a local band.

Life changed when Riley's father went off to fight in the Civil War in 1861. The family (which already included six children) took in an additional orphan child and suffered many hardships. Riley would base his famous poem, *Little Orphant Annie* on this temporary foster sibling (both the child and the poem were named "Allie", but a typesetter made a crucial typo when the poem was finally published).

Riley Senior returned from soldiering a broken man, partially paralyzed and unable to resume his practice. The family was forced to sell their house in town and retreated to the family farm where Riley's mother died in 1870. Riley became estranged from his father at this time and left home. He also started drinking excessively, beginning a life-long habit that would both impact his health and his career.

He embarked on a series of low-paying jobs – house painting, Bible salesman – before starting a sign-painting business in Greenfield. Riley wrote catchy slogans for his signs, in effect, his first published verses. He also started participating in local theatre productions and sending poems to the *Indianapolis Mirror* under the pseudonym "Jay Whit".

When he went to work for the McGrillus Company in Anderson, Indiana shilling tonic medicines in a travelling show that visited small towns around the state, he discovered another calling. Riley both wrote and performed skits promoting the tonics. Eventually, Riley and several friends started a billboard company that became successful enough that he was able to turn to writing in a more committed way, and he returned to Greenfield to do so.

Riley started sending out dozens of poems to newspapers around the country and many of them – the *Danbury News*, the *Indianapolis Journal* and the *Anderson Democrat*, among them – published the verses. At the same time, Riley began to write to prominent American writers, sending poems and requesting their endorsement. He was successful with poet Henry Wadsworth Longfellow who wrote back, "I have read the poems with great pleasure, and I think they show a true poetic faculty and insight." Riley would finally meet Longfellow in person shortly before the latter's death in 1882; he famously wrote about the experience and about Longfellow's profound impact on his work.

The *Anderson Democrat* offered Riley a reporting job in 1877. He took it on while continuing to submit poems at journals and newspapers all over the country. Riley would lose the stability of this reporting job when a prank in which he submitted a poem to a journal claiming it was Edgar Allan Poe's went awry. Spurned by many publishers after this embarrassing incident, Riley joined a travelling lecture circuit and gave poetry readings around the state. A born entertainer, Riley's readings would become hugely popular and remained a primary source of income for most of his life.

Eventually, the Poe debacle faded into the background and the *Indianapolis Journal* relented, hiring Riley as a columnist in 1879; he wrote regularly for them about society affairs while continuing to tour his increasingly theatrical and comedic poetry readings. As his fame increased, Riley dropped his "Jay Whit" pseudonym and wrote under his own name from about 1881.

Around this time Riley began writing what are known as his "Boone County poems". They are almost entirely written in dialect and emphasize rural and agricultural topics, often evoking nostalgia for the simplicity of country life. *The Old Swimmin'-Hole* and *When the Frost Is on the Punkin'* were the most popular, and helped earn the entire series critical acclaim. In 1883, a friend arranged for the private publication of *The Old Swimmin' Hole and 'Leven More Poems'*. The book's popularity dictated a second printing before the end of the year and it continued to sell for years, bolstered by Riley's reading tours.

Riley's prose style lent itself well to public performance. With their emphasis on the natural speech rhythms of mid-western dialects, his most famous poems – *Raggedy Man, Little Orphant Annie* – can look slightly ridiculous on the page. But they come alive when read aloud:

Little Orphant Annie's come to our house to stay,
An' wash the cups an' saucers up, an' brush the crumbs away,
An' shoo the chickens off the porch, an' dust the hearth, an'sweep,
An' make the fire, an' bake the bread, an' earn her board-an'-keep;
An' all us other childern, when the supper-things is done,
We set around the kitchen fire an' has the mostest fun
A-list'nin' to the witch-tales 'at Annie tells about,
An' the Gobble-uns 'at gits you
Ef you
Don't
Watch
Out!

This phenomenon is likely the key to Riley's success with children's verse, as well as the reason he was able to build such fame and fortune on the travelling lecture circuit. It helped also that he was a confident and talented performer.

In 1881 Riley was invited to tour with the Redpath Lyceum Circuit, a prominent series that included writers such as Ralph Waldo Emerson on its roster of regular lecturers. After a successful first season reading in Chicago and Indianapolis, Riley signed a ten-year contract with the Circuit and embarked on a tour of the Eastern seaboard starting in Boston. Riley toured with the Circuit until 1885 when he joined forces with humourist Edgar Wilson Nye. In 1888, the pair co-wrote *Nye and Riley's Railway Guide*, a collection of poems and anecdotes. Nye and Riley also teamed up with another famous American humourist Samuel Clemons (Mark Twain) for joint performances in New York City. Despite contract and agent woes that deprived Riley of his full share of the proceeds, he continued touring with Nye through 1890.

Riley published his third compilation of work in 1888. *Old-Fashioned Roses* was written specifically for the British market and consisted mostly of sonnets; Riley intentionally left his country bumpkin dialects out of this collection. The book was a predictable success in the UK and Riley travelled to Scotland (where he made a pilgrimage to the grave of Robert Burns, a poet with who he is often compared) and England to promote it and conduct readings in 1891.

Back home the next year Riley resumed his lecture and reading tour, teaming up with millionaire author Douglass Sherley for a hugely successful double bill. Coinciding with this, in a savvy and astute cross-promotion, Riley compiled and published perhaps his best-loved book, *Rhymes of Childhood*. It's a work that continues to be popular into the 21st century. It also parted the beginning of the end for Riley's literary reputation. Although he continued to sell out readings in New York and across the US (in fact prospective audience members were often turned away), critics increasingly found his work repetitive and banal. His 1894 verse volume *Armazindy* was very poorly received.

Riley gave his last tour in 1895 and spent his final years in Indianapolis writing patriotic poetry for public recitation on civic occasions (with stirring titles such as *America!* and *The Name of Old Glory*) and poem/elegies for famous friends. His life's work of essays, poems, plays and articles was published in sixteen volumes in 1914.

By this time, Riley was in poor health, weakened by years of heavy drinking. The Hoosier Poet died on July 23, 1916 of a stroke. In a final, unusual tribute, Riley lay in state for a day in the Indiana Statehouse, where thousands came to pay their respects. Not since Lincoln had a public personage received such a send-off. He is buried at Crown Hill Cemetery in Indianapolis.

Riley's legacy is not just a literary one. A wealthy man, he left behind the funding seeds for a number of memorial projects, the James Whitcomb Riley Hospital for Children, Camp Riley for children with disabilities and James Whitcomb Riley House (a museum in which the writer's personal effects and furnishings from his lifetime remain unchanged).

And, as a lasting tribute, the town of Greenfield holds a festival every year in Riley's honor. Every October the "Riley Days" festival opens with a flower parade in which local school children place flowers around the statue of Riley set on the courthouse lawn.

Remembered as both a philanthropist and a poet laureate for the Hoosier state of Indiana, a writer with a distinctive pre-industrial folk ethos and an ear for the humble rhythms of the plain local dialect of the US Midwest, Riley remains to this day a poet of the people.

www.ingramcontent.com/pod-product-compliance
Lightning Source LLC
Chambersburg PA
CBHW061303040426
42444CB00010B/2489